The Manhattan Project

CORNERSTONES OF FREEDOM™

SECOND SERIES

Dan Elish

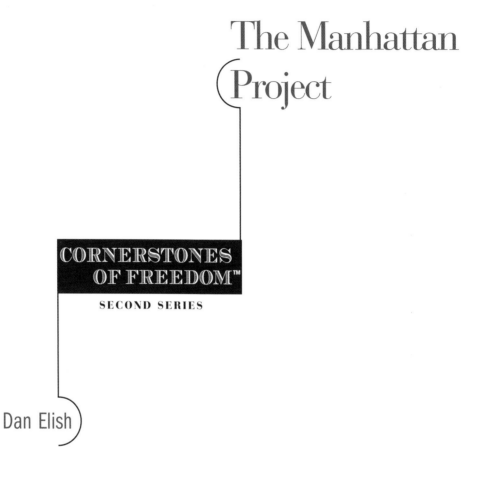

Children's Press®
A Division of Scholastic Inc.
New York • Toronto • London • Auckland • Sydney
Mexico City • New Delhi • Hong Kong
Danbury, Connecticut

Photographs © 2007: Corbis Images: cover top (Bettmann), 20, 27
(Hulton-Deutsh Collection), 40 (Wally McNamee), 6, 12, 16, 18, 21,
25, 26, 28, 32, 33; Getty Images: 11 (Anthony Potter Collection), 9
(Central Press), 29 (Fox Photos), 3, 22 (Fritz Goro/Time Life Pictures),
14, 44 top left (March of Time/Time Life Pictures), 7 (Joe Raedle), 39
(Michael Rougier/Time Life Pictures), 36 (George Silk/Time Life Pictures); National Archives and Records Administration: cover bottom,
4, 19, 30, 31, 45 left; The Art Archive/Picture Desk: 8 (Dagli Orti/Gal-
leria degli Uffizi Florence), 34, 45 right (National Archives Washington
DC); The Image Works: 10, 44 right (Mary Evans Picture Library), 24,
44 bottom left (Topham).

Map by XNR Productions, Inc.

Library of Congress Cataloging-in-Publication Data
Elish, Dan.
  The Manhattan Project / Dan Elish.
     p. cm. — (Cornerstones of freedom. Second series)
  Includes bibliographical references.
  ISBN-13: 978-0-516-23299-7
  ISBN-10: 0-516-23299-1
  1. Manhattan Project (U.S.)—History—Juvenile literature. 2. Atomic
bomb—United States—History—Juvenile literature. I. Title. II. Series.
  QC773.3.U5E35 2007
  355.8'25119097309044—dc22   2006004600

1 2 3 4 5 6 7 8 9 10 R 16 15 14 13 12 11 10 09 08 07

THE DATE WAS MONDAY, JULY 16, 1945. In the northeast corner of the 51,500-acre (20,858-hectare) Alamogordo Bombing and Gunnery Range, in an area known as the Trinity Site, stood a 100-foot (30-meter) steel tower. Hanging near the top was the world's first atomic bomb, known to the men who built it as "the gadget." For almost four years, the United States had been at war against Germany and Japan.

A steel container called Jumbo, designed to hold the atomic bomb, is put into position at the Trinity Site.

While American troops were among the forces fighting in Europe and the South Pacific, a group of the world's greatest scientists were stationed in Los Alamos, New Mexico. They were working on what came to be called the Manhattan Project. Their mission was to build a bomb so destructive it would end the war. For two and a half years, these brilliant men worked eighteen-hour days, constructing an atomic bomb. Now it was time to test it.

After a delay caused by a thunderstorm, Manhattan Project director General Leslie Groves gave the order: the gadget would be tested at 5:30 in the morning. **Ground zero** was quickly evacuated while the leading scientists moved into three observation **bunkers** 10,000 yards (9,144 m) away. At 5:10 A.M., "The Star-Spangled Banner" played over a public-address system. Most of

This map shows in red the places where the atomic bomb was used.

the scientists moved 10 miles (16 kilometers) away and watched nervously. Others watched from Compania Hill, 20 miles (32 km) away. After all, no one knew exactly what would happen when the bomb exploded. Some scientists worried that the bomb would ignite the atmosphere and blow up the world. Others worried it wouldn't work at all.

Then it happened—an awe-inspiring explosion. Physicists, scientists who study **matter** and energy, were at the observation bunkers. One of them remembered, "Suddenly, there was an enormous flash of light, the brightest light I have ever seen. . . . [T]here was an enormous ball of fire which grew and grew . . . a new thing had been born."

Later, it was calculated that the world's first atomic bomb exploded with the force of about 18,000 tons of TNT. The bomb was so powerful that it blew out windows 120 miles (193 km) away. At ground zero, it left a 300-foot (91-m)-wide crater.

One of the men watching was J. Robert Oppenheimer, the scientific head of the Manhattan Project. When Oppenheimer saw the mushroom cloud bloom over the New Mexico desert, he thought of a line from an ancient Hindu poem, the "Bhagavad Gita": "Now, I am become Death, destroyer of worlds."

Members of the Manhattan Project look over a map of the Trinity Site.

* * * *

The world's first atomic bomb explodes on July 16, 1945.

SPLITTING THE ATOM

Constructing the first atomic bomb was one of the great scientific and engineering feats in world history. But it would not have been possible without an important series of scientific discoveries that had occurred during the preceding forty years.

At the turn of the twentieth century, scientists knew that particles called **atoms** were the building blocks of all matter. The famous scientist Sir Isaac Newton, who lived from 1643 until 1727, theorized that atoms were like marbles. They were solid and hard and could not be divided.

As it turned out, Newton was wrong. Research in the early 1900s showed that atoms were not solid at all. Rather, they were made up of particles called **electrons**, **protons**, and **neu-**

HOTTER THAN THE SUN

When the first atomic bomb exploded at the Trinity Site, the temperature at ground zero was estimated to be 100,000,000 degrees Fahrenheit (55,559,982 degrees Celsius). This is three times the temperature in the interior of the sun. The bomb's mushroom cloud reached 41,000 feet (12,500 m) into the sky. This is higher than Mount Everest, the tallest mountain on Earth.

Isaac Newton was responsible for many major scientific advances.

E = mc^2

Albert Einstein was the most important scientist of the twentieth century. In 1905, he wrote a famous equation that would change the world: E = mc^2. This means that energy is equal to mass times the square of the speed of light. In other words, Einstein discovered that all matter contains massive amounts of untapped energy. The scientists at Los Alamos used Einstein's discovery to make the first atomic bomb.

trons. At the center of each atom was the **nucleus**, which was made up of protons and neutrons. One or more electrons orbited around the nucleus. Scientists also discovered that the protons had a positive charge and the electrons had a negative charge.

In 1938, Austrian scientists Lise Meitner and Otto Frisch, her nephew, made a dramatic discovery about the nature of atoms. By bombarding the **element uranium** with neutrons, they realized they could split the nucleus of an atom. When the nucleus split into pieces, it released neutrons and protons. Most exciting, it also released energy. Meitner and Frisch called this process **fission**.

Soon scientists around the world were talking about it. What if the energy of a single split atom could split two more atoms? What if billions of atoms split at the same time? A tremendous new source of energy would be created. The famous scientist Enrico Fermi said, "A little bomb like that and [the world] would disappear."

THE RISE OF ADOLF HITLER

Under any circumstances, the discovery of nuclear fission would have been greeted with great interest by the world's scientists. But events in Europe made the discovery even more important and potentially very dangerous.

In 1918, Germany had lost World War I, which began in 1914. As part of the peace treaty that followed, Germany was not allowed to rearm and was forced to pay enormous sums of money to Britain, France, and the other victorious countries. As a result, in the 1920s, the German economy collapsed. Struggling Germans began to follow a powerful and frightening new leader: Adolf Hitler.

As Hitler rose to power, he proposed reuniting Austria and Germany into a nation made up of Aryans, or people native to Western Europe. He also promised Germans a

★ ★ ★ ★

Adolf Hitler greets admirers in Nuremberg, Germany, in 1933.

**SCIENCE FICTION—
OR SCIENCE FACT?**

In 1914, more than thirty years before the first atomic bomb was exploded, the great science-fiction writer H. G. Wells published a book called *The World Set Free*. Wells predicted a future in which a war was fought with atomic weapons.

return to the days when their country was strong and their economy was booming. In 1933, Hitler became Germany's chancellor, or head of state. He closed down newspapers and proclaimed that only Aryans could be public employees. All political parties except his own Nazi Party were declared illegal.

Hitler hated Jewish people. In 1933, he proclaimed a one-day boycott of Jewish businesses. Jewish children were no longer allowed to go to certain schools. Two years later, the Nuremberg Laws stripped Jews of German citizenship. Soon signs saying JEWS NOT WELCOME appeared in many German cities.

Hitler targeted other groups as well. Romanies, Catholics, homosexuals, the disabled, and the mentally ill were also victims in his plan to create an Aryan society.

A Nazi soldier stands outside a Jewish-owned store in Berlin. The sign reads, "Germans! Defend yourselves! Don't buy from Jews!"

Leó Szilárd wanted to warn President Roosevelt.

By 1938, Germany invaded Austria, and Hitler's ultimate goal had become clear: to conquer Europe and exterminate the world's Jewish population. In 1939, when Hitler invaded Poland, France and Britain declared war on Germany.

As German troops spread across Europe, many Jewish scientists were terrified. Albert Einstein and others had fled Germany in the mid-1930s. But what about the scientists who remained loyal to Hitler? What if they knew about nuclear fission? What if Hitler was working on an atomic bomb?

WARNING ROOSEVELT

Elected in 1932, President Franklin D. Roosevelt had helped steer the United States during the **Great Depression**, the worst economic crisis in the country's history. Toward the end of the 1930s, Roosevelt was concerned about the rise of Adolf Hitler. When Britain and France were drawn into war against Germany, Roosevelt wanted to help defeat Hitler. But with the horrors of World War I still fresh in people's minds, most Americans had no interest in fighting another bloody European war. With public opinion against him, Roosevelt sent Britain and France supplies to help them fight the war. In the meantime, he did what he could to get the United States ready to enter the war when the time came.

By 1939, Hungarian-born physicist Leó Szilárd had escaped to the United States from Europe. Szilárd joined forces with two other Hungarian scientists, Eugene Wigner and Edward Teller. "The Hungarian conspiracy," as they were later called, agreed that they had to warn President Roosevelt right away about the possibility of atomic weapons. But they did not know how they would get the president's attention. Even though Szilárd was a well-known scientist in Europe, it was almost certain that Roosevelt had not heard of him. But there was one scientist the president

FERMI ESCAPES

In the 1930s, Enrico Fermi was one of the world's leading physicists. His wife was Jewish. In 1938, when Fermi was awarded the Nobel Prize in Physics, it gave him the chance to leave Italy, a country that had joined forces with Germany. After accepting the award, Fermi and his family moved to New York City. Eventually, he became one of the leading scientists on the Manhattan Project.

★ ★ ★ ★

Albert Einstein was the most influential scientist of the twentieth century. Without his help, the "Hungarian conspiracy" may not have been successful at warning President Roosevelt of the danger of atomic weapons in the wrong hands.

of the United States would listen to: Albert Einstein.

On July 16, 1939, Szilárd and Wigner visited Einstein at his summer home in Long Island, New York. Einstein immediately understood the terrifying potential of fission and agreed to write a letter, dated August 2, 1939, to Roosevelt. Later, Szilárd wrote, "The one thing most scientists are really afraid of is to make fools of themselves. Einstein was free from such fear and this above all is what made his position unique on this occasion."

It was agreed that the letter would be delivered by Alexander Sachs, one of Roosevelt's friends. With events spiraling out of control in Europe, it took Sachs a few months to get an appointment with Roosevelt. Finally, on October 11, 1939, Sachs met with the president in the White House. Sachs started the meeting with a story. More than a hundred years earlier, there had been a young inventor who had written to Napoléon Bonaparte. This inventor claimed that he could help Napoléon defeat Britain by building a fleet of ships that didn't need sails. Napoléon was unimpressed. As it turned out, the young inventor was Robert Fulton, the inventor of the steamboat.

This story helped Sachs get Roosevelt's attention. Sachs then told the president about fission and gave him Einstein's letter. As the story goes, Roosevelt called his chief aide and said, "This requires action!"

BELGIAN URANIUM

Toward the end of the 1930s, the world's largest uranium mines were in the Belgian Congo in Africa. Leó Szilárd and other scientists were worried that Germany, which had already conquered Belgium, would soon control the mines, giving them all the uranium they would need to build an atomic bomb. However, Belgian authorities were able to ship most of their uranium to the United States before the Germans found it.

**Italian nuclear physicist
Enrico Fermi**

THE FIRST CHAIN REACTION

Following the meeting with Alexander Sachs, Roosevelt set
up the Advisory Committee on Uranium. Szilárd asked for
$6,000 to construct an experiment that would hopefully pro-
duce a nuclear **chain reaction**. It was a crucial first step:
without such a chain reaction, there could be no atomic
bomb. Although the project was funded, atomic research

16

was not yet a priority for the U.S. government. A man named Dr. Lyman J. Briggs, who had oversight of the uranium committee, didn't fully trust foreign scientists. Work moved forward slowly.

But it wasn't long before events overseas gave a push to American experiments with fission. In 1940, France surrendered to German forces. Britain was being bombed by the Germans almost daily. Then on December 7, 1941, Japan launched a devastating sneak attack on the U.S. Navy's Pacific Fleet stationed at Pearl Harbor, Hawaii. Within a week, the United States entered World War II on two fronts: in Europe against Germany and Italy, and in the South Pacific against Japan.

Meanwhile, Enrico Fermi became the first scientist to determine if a self-sustaining chain reaction was possible. With the help of another $40,000 from the federal government, he staged an experiment beneath Stagg Field stadium at the University of Chicago.

Fermi and his team constructed a pile of 400 tons of graphite, 6 tons of uranium metal, and 50 tons of uranium oxide. On December 2, 1942, forty scientists came to watch. That morning, Fermi ordered that a series of control rods be slowly pulled out of the pile. A control rod is a rod that is made of chemical elements that control the rate of decay of uranium and **plutonium**. When removed from the central core of a nuclear reactor, the control rod allows a chain reaction to begin. At 3:36 P.M., the last rods were removed. The fission reaction was self-sustaining, which means it was able to continue by itself. Left uncontrolled, the reaction would have

This is one of the layers of the pile that became the world's first nuclear reactor, constructed by Fermi and his team at the University of Chicago.

FATEFUL WORDS

After Enrico Fermi's successful test producing a self-sustaining nuclear reaction, scientist Leó Szilárd was worried. Even though he had been the one to ask Albert Einstein to warn President Roosevelt of the awesome power of nuclear weapons, he told Fermi, "This day will go down as a black day in the history of mankind."

grown, killing Fermi and his team, as well as releasing radiation into downtown Chicago. But at 3:53 in the afternoon, Fermi ordered the control rod reinserted into the pile. The reaction stopped. One of the scientists called Washington, D.C., to report the good news.

"The Italian navigator has just landed in the New World," he said, in code.

"Were the natives friendly?" was the reply.

"Everyone landed safe and happy."

Having proved that a self-sustaining nuclear reaction was possible, the United States had taken a giant leap forward in its quest to develop an atomic bomb.

GROVES AND OPPENHEIMER

By the time Enrico Fermi had successfully produced a nuclear chain reaction, the atomic bomb program had been given a name. Since its first offices had been in Manhattan, in New York City, the project was called the Manhattan Project. And now that the country was at war, the government began to take the program more seriously. By the summer of 1942, the secretary of war, George Marshall, realized that the program needed a strong leader. He picked a colonel in the Army Corps of Engineers named Leslie Richard Groves.

Groves was a large, forceful man who wanted to be overseas, fighting in Europe. He had no desire to stay in the United States to supervise a bunch of scientists while they tried to build a bomb that might not even work. "If you do the job right," he was told, "it will win the war." Groves remained unimpressed with the project, even after he was promoted to general.

Still, Groves turned out to be the right man for the job. An expert organizer who could bully his way into getting what he needed, he skillfully pulled together the different pieces of the project. He was also smart enough to realize that he needed help. While he was a superb military officer, he

Leslie R. Groves

19

J. Robert Oppenheimer

GENERAL GROVES

At the time of the Manhattan Project, General Leslie Richard Groves was known throughout the army to be extremely tough. One man remembered him this way: "He had absolute confidence in his decisions and he was absolutely ruthless in how he approached a problem to get it done. . . . I've often thought that if I were to [do it] over again, I would select Groves as boss."

didn't pretend to know anything about science. Clearly, the Manhattan Project needed a coleader, someone to oversee the scientists who would build the actual bomb.

Though there were many capable scientists in the country, some were already working on different parts of the war effort, such as improving battle weapons. So Groves chose J. Robert Oppenheimer, a thirty-eight-year-old graduate of Harvard University who had worked with some of the world's greatest scientists. Oppenheimer specialized in a branch of physics known as quantum theory. A brilliant man, Oppenheimer spoke six languages and could read Sanskrit, the ancient language of the Hindus.

Groves (left) and Oppenheimer differed from each other in many ways, but they cooperated to reach the goal of building an atomic weapon.

Groves and Oppenheimer made an unlikely team. While Groves was large, Oppenheimer, or "Oppie," as many called him, was thin. Groves didn't smoke or drink; Oppenheimer was said to smoke five packs of cigarettes a day. Groves was the son of a chaplain; Oppenheimer was Jewish. Still, they worked well together. Over time, Groves developed a deep respect for Oppenheimer, saying, "He's a genius. . . . Why, Oppenheimer knows about everything."

As director of the Manhattan Project, Groves (shown here at the Trinity Site) respected Oppenheimer's intelligence.

MOVING TO LOS ALAMOS

The first thing Groves and Oppenheimer agreed on was that they needed a place where the scientists could work. As a boy, Oppenheimer had spent time in the Southwest. He once said, "My two great loves are physics and desert country. It's a pity they can't be combined." Now he had his chance.

The Los Alamos Ranch School was located on an isolated stretch of land, high in the desert mountains, 30 miles (48 km) southeast of Santa Fe, New Mexico. Most of its students were the sons of wealthy families from the East. In financial trouble, the owners of the school sold it to the U.S. Army in November 1942. A month later, more than 3,000 workers arrived to build laboratories and dorms.

Oppenheimer's first task was to attract the best talent in the country to the site. For months, he traveled the country, convincing scientists to move to Los Alamos. It was a difficult job. At that point, the bomb, or "the gadget," as the people at Los Alamos called it, was top secret. Oppenheimer had to persuade men with comfortable jobs as university professors to drop everything and join him in a place he wasn't allowed to identify to work on a project he wasn't allowed to describe. One scientist remembered, "I thought [Oppenheimer] had a screw loose somewhere."

But Oppenheimer was able to convince scientists to join him in his work by reminding them of the importance of preventing a German victory in the war. Oppenheimer was also

THE MIDDLE OF NOWHERE

During World War II, Los Alamos was not well known, and people seldom traveled there. The sudden flurry of train tickets purchased in Princeton, New Jersey, for travel to New Mexico surprised the stationmaster there, who questioned what was happening. No one, however, could give him an answer.

Scientists meet with Groves (center) to discuss progress on the development of the atomic bomb.

Los Alamos grew into the site of a national laboratory.

able to promise the scientists a chance to work on cutting-edge science with the best minds in the country. On April 15, 1943, with fifty scientists ready to work, the Manhattan Project officially began.

URANIUM AND PLUTONIUM

Before the scientists at Los Alamos could even think about making an atomic bomb they needed to gather the two known elements in the world that would trigger a nuclear reaction.

25

TOP SECRET

The employees at Oak Ridge and Hanford worked under tight security. Thousands of men and women toiled day and night and were never told why their work was so important.

The first was called uranium 235. The second was called plutonium 239. In 1942, when General Groves took over the Manhattan Project, the amount of plutonium in the world was so small it could be placed on the head of a pin. The amount of uranium 235 was almost equally small.

Gathering enough of these two extremely rare substances was an almost overwhelming challenge. To do it, Groves asked the government for money to build two enormous factories.

The first was in Oak Ridge, Tennessee. One thousand homes were also built to house 50,000 workers. Their job was to separate uranium 235 from the more common uranium 238. But it was a nearly impossible task. Uranium 238 contains three more neutrons than uranium 235 and is slightly heavier. Workers used giant machines called cyclotrons to

The uranium factory at Oak Ridge, Tennessee

26

A view of the plutonium factory near Hanford, Washington

spin uranium 238 extremely fast. Over time, the lighter uranium 235 gathered on the outside of the cyclotron. Still, it was a painstaking process. Three years later, at war's end, the Oak Ridge factory had produced only enough uranium 235 to build one bomb.

While work was progressing at Oak Ridge, Groves focused on a second giant factory near Hanford, Washington. This one would produce plutonium. This operation, too, was top secret.

* * * *

In just a few months, 45,000 workers built Hanford into the fourth-largest city in Washington State. Production began on September 26, 1944, and the Hanford reactor produced its first plutonium on November 6. The plutonium was refined and shipped to Oppenheimer at Los Alamos on February 5, 1945. Oppenheimer's team received enough material to make three bombs. One would be triggered by uranium; the other two would use plutonium. Now they had to find a way to make them work.

WORKING AT LOS ALAMOS

Manhattan Project scientists lived in these simple cabins.

Building an atomic bomb would have been hard enough in the cleanest, most modern laboratories in the country. But the scientists at Los Alamos had to make do with more outdated living and working conditions. Scientists lived in hastily constructed cabins, which were unheated—even in winter—and walked down dirt streets. There were only five bathtubs. Clean drinking water was scarce. In fact, it wasn't uncommon to turn on a tap and have worms come out of the faucet.

Many of the scientists who developed the atomic bomb gathered for this photo. They include Enrico Fermi (seated, second from right) and Edward Teller (standing, first on left).

Even so, the scientists adapted to their surroundings as best they could. There were parties, two dance bands, a soda fountain, and a radio station. Scientist Edward Teller shipped in his piano and played Beethoven late into the night. By all accounts, Oppenheimer succeeded at making Los Alamos an exciting and even fun place to be.

By 1944, Los Alamos was a walled city of 6,000 people. The task of turning a nuclear chain reaction into a workable bomb was enormous. Scientists and mathematicians worked in seven divisions: theoretical physics, exploratory physics, **ordnance**, explosives, bomb physics, chemistry, and **metallurgy**. Part of Oppenheimer's great genius was that he was able to understand and comment on every detail of the bomb. Along with his mastery of

A GERMAN BOMB?

During the war, the United States and Great Britain did everything they could to find out whether the Germans were building their own atomic bomb. Several bombings were ordered on a German-controlled factory in Norway that General Groves and others suspected of producing heavy water, a substance needed to produce a nuclear reaction. It wasn't discovered until near the end of the war that the Germans weren't as close to constructing their own nuclear weapon as many feared.

The Little Boy atomic bomb

the science involved in creating it, he was an excellent team leader. Oppenheimer was able to keep everyone working together toward the goal: to produce a bomb before Germany did and use it to end the war.

One thing Oppenheimer didn't have to do was convince people to work. Most nights, the labs would be busy until midnight or later. For most of the war, the citizens of Santa Fe had no real idea what the scientists at Los Alamos were working on. Some thought it was a poison gas factory. Oppenheimer and other scientists deliberately spread the rumor that they were working on a new electric rocket. In fact, secrecy was so tight that some wives of scientists living at Los Alamos didn't even know what their husbands were doing.

As work progressed on the two different bombs, scientists came to have more confidence in the one that used uranium 235. This bomb could be set off by firing a lump of uranium into a uranium target at a speed of 2,000 feet (610 m) per second. This would cause a chain reaction and an atomic explosion. Because this bomb was long and thin, it was called Thin Man. When the size of the bomb was reduced, its name was changed to Little Boy.

A scientist marks a Little Boy bomb number L-11. (This bomb was later dropped on Hiroshima, Japan.)

On the other hand, the bomb that used plutonium was more difficult. The method used to set off the uranium bomb would not work because the two masses of plutonium required to create a nuclear reaction could not be brought together quickly enough to avoid an explosion that occurred too soon. Instead, the plutonium had to be surrounded by explosives, which would trigger it to be set off. But there was a problem: the blast wave of a typical explosion moves outward. A physicist named Seth Neddermeyer discovered a way to make an explosion move inward, or to implode. Still, it was very difficult to achieve. Though Oppenheimer believed the uranium bomb would explode, he and others thought the plutonium bomb would need to be tested.

31

The 100-foot (30-m) steel tower from which the first atomic bomb was dropped

JUMBO

Initially, scientists weren't sure if the bomb would explode, so they decided to house it in a 214-ton steel container they called Jumbo. That way, if the bomb didn't explode, they would be able to save the valuable and rare plutonium. Though Jumbo was moved by railroad to the Trinity Site in April 1945, the scientists eventually decided that it wasn't needed.

THE TRINITY TEST

The search for the best place to test the bomb began as early as June 1944. The area had to be flat, have good weather, and be located far from population centers. After visiting a number of sites, an area called Jornada del Muerto was chosen. In English, the name means "journey of death." Oppenheimer called it Trinity.

By November, workmen were getting the site ready for the test, building huge concrete bunkers along with the 100-foot (30-m) steel tower that would house the gadget. Back at Los Alamos, scientists worked even harder preparing for the test. Always thin, Oppenheimer lost even more weight from the strain of working eighteen-hour days. During time away from the lab, scientists helped to make face masks to wear during the test.

In April 1945, Oak Ridge finally produced enough uranium to build a single bomb. It was shipped to Los Alamos. At the same time, the men working on the plutonium bomb were also making great progress. But then, just as scientists were closing in on finishing the bombs, something shocking happened.

On April 12, while vacationing in Georgia, President Roosevelt died. The new president was Harry S. Truman. A day after being sworn in, he was told about the bomb. Then

Jumbo, the container for the bomb, as it was being transported to the Trinity Site

on May 8, 1945, Germany surrendered. The Manhattan Project had been designed to stop Adolf Hitler. Still, even with Nazi Germany defeated, Oppenheimer and the workers at Los Alamos didn't seriously consider calling off their test. The United States was still at war with Japan, an enemy who seemed determined not to surrender. Also, the Manhattan Project had helped end the Great Depression in the United States. Three new towns—Los Alamos, Oak Ridge, and Hanford—had been built, and thousands of people were working toward making an atomic bomb. A test site had been prepared. General Groves did not want to stop the project without finding out if the bomb worked.

The mushroom cloud rises into the sky following the explosion at the Trinity Site.

There was also the matter of the Soviet Union. The Soviets had been allies of the United States in the war against Germany. But now that the war was over, Soviet leader Joseph Stalin clearly wanted to control Eastern Europe. Churchill, Stalin, and Truman, called the Big Three, were set to begin meeting in Potsdam, Germany, on July 15, 1945, to discuss the postwar world. U.S. leaders believed that Truman would be able to **negotiate** with more confidence if he knew that the United States had an atomic bomb.

So on the morning of July 16, 1945, the scientists at Los Alamos gathered at the Trinity Site. At exactly forty-five seconds after 5:29 A.M., the first atomic bomb exploded, changing the world forever.

HIROSHIMA

In Potsdam, on July 21, Truman received a message from General Groves: "The test was successful beyond the most optimistic expectations of anyone."

Truman was thrilled. He had entered the meeting with Stalin, hoping to convince the Soviet dictator to enter the war against Japan—a move that might have led to Soviet control of part of Japan, as well as Eastern Europe. Now Truman had the means to end the war in the Pacific without Soviet help.

Japan refused to surrender. After a series of bloody battles that claimed thousands of lives, Americans had captured island after island in the South Pacific, moving closer to Japan. The main islands of Japan had been bombed repeatedly from the air, killing about one million Japanese. Still, Japan vowed to fight on. Some American generals predicted

OPPENHEIMER AND THE UNITED NATIONS

Even after Germany surrendered, Oppenheimer believed that the United States should finish making the atomic bomb. In 1945, the United Nations was being formed. Oppenheimer thought that the world should know about the bomb so nuclear secrets could be shared among all nations.

A view of Hiroshima, Japan, shows the devastated city after the atomic bomb was dropped from the *Enola Gay*.

that repeated bombing would eventually force Japan to quit. But most military leaders thought that the only way to win would be to invade the Japanese mainland, an operation that would probably cost as many as one million American dead and wounded.

However, with the uranium bomb Little Boy ready to go, President Truman could now drop an atomic bomb. Some suggested that the United States set up a demonstration of the bomb's awesome power for officials of the Japanese government. But others worried how it would look if Little Boy didn't explode. So Truman prepared to give the order to drop the bomb on a civilian, or nonmilitary, target. On July 26,

1945, the United States and Great Britain demanded Japan's immediate and unconditional surrender or face destruction. Soon after, an American warship, the USS *Indianapolis*, delivered Little Boy to the Tinian Airfield on Tinian Island in the Northern Mariana Islands. Tinian was the United States airfield closest to Japan. On July 28, Japan announced that it would not surrender. A day later, a Japanese submarine sank the *Indianapolis*, killing 880 Americans.

Hiroshima was a Japanese city that had been spared from the repeated bombings that had already taken place. It was chosen as the city that Little Boy would be dropped on so that the power of the atomic bomb would be clear to the Japanese government.

At 2:45 on the morning of August 6, 1945, Colonel Paul Tibbets and his crew took off from the Tinian Airfield in the *Enola Gay*, a B-29 airplane he had named for his mother. At 9:10 A.M., Tibbets circled over Hiroshima. At 9:15, flying 6 miles (9.7 km) over the city, he released the bomb from the plane's cargo area. It exploded with a light so bright it could have been seen from another planet. Though the blast lasted only nine seconds, it left more than 100,000 people dead, 40,000 injured, and 20,000 missing. Survivors suffered burns and blindness. Many contracted radiation sickness. Excessive exposure leads to symptoms that can include nausea, fatigue, infection, and cancer. Indeed, the victims of Hiroshima suffered for years and the death toll continued to climb.

A SPY AT LOS ALAMOS

To the other scientists at Los Alamos, Klaus Fuchs seemed to be a quiet, hard worker. Only after the war was it discovered that he had been a spy for the Soviet government, passing atomic secrets to them. At the end of the war, Fuchs was sentenced to fourteen years in prison. It is believed that Fuchs's help made it possible for the Soviets to make their own atomic bombs.

"OPPIE" ARGUES FOR PEACE

After the war, J. Robert Oppenheimer argued against the spread of nuclear weapons, saying, "The only hope for our future safety must lie in [cooperation] based on confidence and good faith with the other peoples of the world."

At first, the Japanese government didn't believe what had happened. They still refused to surrender. On August 9, the second nuclear bomb, Fat Man, was dropped on the city of Nagasaki. Eighty thousand Japanese were killed. The next day, Japan finally surrendered.

THE NUCLEAR AGE

After the end of World War II, J. Robert Oppenheimer became an American celebrity, known as the brilliant man who built the bomb. However, the end of the war did not bring a final peace to the world. The Soviet Union moved quickly and gained control over most of Eastern Europe. In 1949, the Soviets exploded their own atomic bomb. Americans were shocked and scared.

The early 1950s in the United States were marked by a great fear of the Soviet Union and their system of government, called communism. Communism is a way of organizing a country so that all the land, houses, and businesses belong to the government. U.S. senator Joseph McCarthy began to accuse well-respected Americans of being communists. Many loyal Americans were thrown out of government and were unable to work for years.

One of those Americans was Oppenheimer. After the end of the war, Oppenheimer argued that the United States should share its atomic secrets with other nations. Many people disagreed. Scientist Edward Teller argued that the United States should build a hydrogen bomb. This bomb would have one

U.S. senator Joseph McCarthy speaks out against the activities of Americans accused of being communists.

hundred times the power of the one that destroyed Hiroshima. Oppenheimer thought it was a terrible idea.

As the fear of communism swept the nation, some Americans became suspicious of Oppenheimer's past associations with communist groups. In 1954, he was accused of being a risk to the United States. For a man who had come to enjoy

U.S. president Ronald Reagan (left) and Soviet leader Mikhail Gorbachev met in the Oval Office of the White House in December 1987 after signing an agreement to limit the number of their countries' nuclear weapons.

working in government and who believed strongly that nuclear weapons should be limited, it was a cruel blow. He spent the rest of his life as director of the Institute for Advanced Studies at Princeton University in New Jersey and died in 1967.

The decades after World War II were marked by a cold war between the United States and the Soviet Union. No shots were fired on a battlefield, but both countries poured massive amounts of money into building more and bigger nuclear weapons. In 1962, the United States and the Soviet Union came close to nuclear war over a dispute involving Soviet missile sites in Cuba. However, in the early 1970s, Soviet and American leaders began to agree to limit the numbers of nuclear weapons. In the late 1980s, President Ronald Reagan and Soviet leader Mikhail Gorbachev agreed to destroy some of their nuclear weapons.

A LASTING IMPACT

The Manhattan Project remains one of the greatest scientific and engineering triumphs in the history of the world. General Leslie Groves and J. Robert Oppenheimer and the scientists at Los Alamos achieved the near impossible for a just cause: ending World War II. Even so, the world must now live with the powerful weapons that were created. Today, the United States, Russia, and the other countries that made up the Soviet Union are no longer enemies. But that doesn't mean the world is safe from the terrible power of nuclear weapons. It is up to people everywhere to work together to ensure that nuclear weapons are never misused in wartime, or used to destroy peace where it exists in the world.

Glossary

atoms—tiny particles that make up the universe

bunkers—underground shelters

chain reaction—a chemical or nuclear event that makes energy, which causes further events of the same kind

electrons—tiny particles that move around the nucleus of an atom; electrons have a negative electrical charge

element—a substance that cannot be split

fission—the process of splitting atoms, which gives off energy

Great Depression—the period in the United States from 1929 until the 1940s when unemployment and poverty were high

ground zero—the point where a nuclear explosion occurs

matter—anything that has weight and takes up space; matter can be a solid, a liquid, or a gas

metallurgy—the science and technology of metals

negotiate—to bargain or to discuss something so that an agreement can be made

neutrons—tiny particles in the nucleus of an atom; neutrons have no electrical charge

nucleus—the central part of an atom, made up of neutrons, protons, and electrons

ordnance—military supplies, including weapons, ammunition, combat vehicles, and tools and equipment

plutonium—an element made from uranium

protons—tiny particles in the nucleus of an atom; protons have a positive electrical charge

Soviet Union—the former federation of fifteen republics including Russia, Ukraine, and other nations of Eastern Europe and northern Asia

uranium—a radioactive metal that is the main source of nuclear energy

Timeline: The

1905

Albert Einstein publishes his theory that $E = mc^2$.

1938

Austrian scientists Lise Meitner and Otto Frisch discover nuclear fission.

1939

JULY 16
Leó Szilárd convinces Albert Einstein to write a letter to U.S. president Franklin D. Roosevelt.

OCTOBER 11
Alexander Sachs meets with U.S. president Roosevelt to warn him of the potential of nuclear fission.

1941

DECEMBER 7
Japan attacks the U.S. naval base at Pearl Harbor, Hawaii.

DECEMBER 11
Germany declares war on the United States.

DECEMBER 8
The United States declares war on Japan.

Manhattan Project

1942

DECEMBER 2
Enrico Fermi creates the first self-sustaining nuclear chain reaction.

1943

APRIL 15
The Manhattan Project officially begins.

1945

MAY 8
Germany surrenders.

JULY 16
The first atomic bomb, nicknamed "the gadget," is exploded.

AUGUST 6
Uranium bomb Little Boy is dropped on the Japanese city of Hiroshima.

AUGUST 9
Plutonium bomb Fat Man is dropped on the Japanese city of Nagasaki.

AUGUST 10
Japan surrenders.

1949

The Soviet Union explodes its first atomic bomb.

1953

The United States explodes the world's first hydrogen bomb.

To Find Out More

BOOKS

Cohen, Daniel. *The Manhattan Project*. Brookfield, Conn.: Twenty-First Century Books, 1999.

Gonzales, Doreen. *The Manhattan Project and the Atomic Bomb*. Berkeley Heights, N.J.: Enslow Publishers, Inc., 2000.

Tracy, Kathleen. *Top Secret: The Story of the Manhattan Project*. Hockessin, DE: Mitchell Lane Publishers, 2005.

ONLINE SITES

The Manhattan Project: An Interactive History
http://www.mbe.doe.gov/me70/manhattan/index.htm

Manhattan Project Heritage Preservation Association
http://www.childrenofthemanhattanproject.org/

National Atomic Museum
http://www.atomicmuseum.com/tour/manhattanproject.cfm

Index

Bold numbers indicate illustrations.

About the Author

Dan Elish is the author of numerous books for children, including *The Worldwide Dessert Contest* and *Born Too Short: The Confessions of an Eighth-Grade Basket Case*, which was picked as a 2003 book for the Teen Age by the New York Public Library. For the Cornerstones of Freedom series, he has also written *The Black Sox Scandal of 1919* and *The Supreme Court*. He lives in New York City with his wife and two children.